EARTH'S PRECIOUS

WATER

AN ESSENTIAL NATURAL RESOURCE

by Joy Gregory

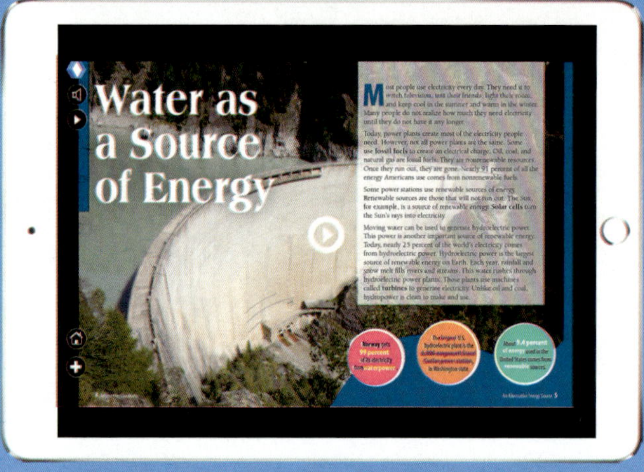

Lightbox is an all-inclusive digital solution for the teaching and learning of curriculum topics in an original, groundbreaking way. Lightbox is based on National Curriculum Standards.

STANDARD FEATURES OF LIGHTBOX

AUDIO High-quality narration using text-to-speech system

ACTIVITIES Printable PDFs that can be emailed and graded

SLIDESHOWS Pictorial overviews of key concepts

VIDEOS Embedded high-definition video clips

WEBLINKS Curated links to external, child-safe resources

TRANSPARENCIES Step-by-step layering of maps, diagrams, charts, and timelines

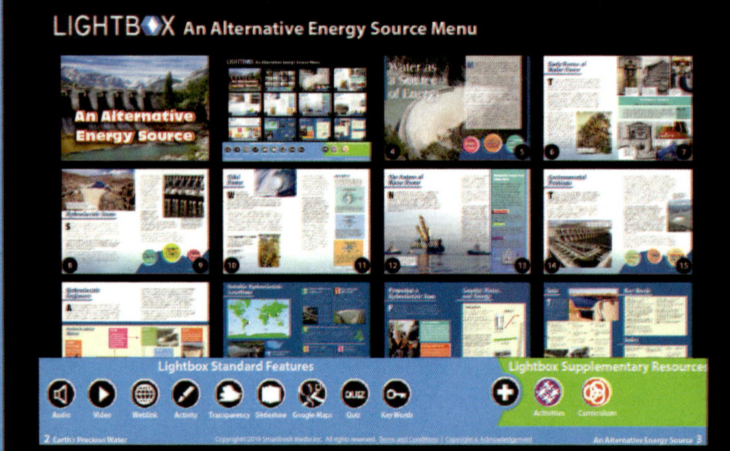

INTERACTIVE MAPS Interactive maps and aerial satellite imagery

QUIZZES Ten multiple choice questions that are automatically graded and emailed for teacher assessment

KEY WORDS Matching key concepts to their definitions

Contents

What Is Water?

Water is one of Earth's simplest chemical compounds. To be a compound, a chemical must include at least two different **elements**. Water is a chemical compound because every **molecule** of water includes the elements hydrogen and oxygen. The chemical formula of water is H_20. It means every molecule of water has two **atoms** of hydrogen and one atom of oxygen.

The chemical simplicity of water disguises three important facts about this compound. First, water is one of the most important substances on Earth. This **transparent**, odorless and tasteless substance is essential for plant and animal life. When scientists study other planets, they look for evidence of water. If there are no signs of water on that planet, that planet is unlikely to support life.

The second most-important fact about water is that it is one of the most abundant substances on Earth. More than 70 percent of Earth's surface is covered by water in its liquid form. In its other forms, water can freeze to form ice on a pond, or "vaporize" to create fog or rainclouds. This ability to exist in three different forms is the third most-compelling fact about water. Together, these facts make water one of the most interesting chemical compounds on the planet. Water supports life, it is found all over the planet, and its ability to exist in three forms provides people with all kinds of opportunities to live, work, and play.

A **person** can **live up to** about **one week without** water.

The **human adult body** is about **60 percent** water.

If **all of Earth's glaciers melted**, oceans would rise about **230 feet** (70 meters).

Forms of Water

Water is the only substance on Earth that can be found naturally in three different states. Water exists as a liquid, gas, or solid because its physical properties change with the temperature. The Celsius temperature scale used by many scientists is based on the fact that water boils at 100 degrees Celsius (212 degrees Fahrenheit) and freezes at 0°C (32°F). Since water can take on a large amount of heat before it boils, its liquid form cools plants, animals, and machines, such as radiators.

The density, or amount of molecules in a certain space, of water changes when it changes its physical form. As a gas, water is not very dense. This allows water vapor to float. As solid ice, water expands to take up 9 percent more space than it would as a liquid. Ice floats because ice is less dense than liquid water. These changes are important in nature. When water **evaporates** and becomes a gas, that gas can move great distances through the atmosphere before falling back to Earth as rain or snow. When the surface of a pond or lake freezes, the ice above **insulates** the rest of the water and keeps it warm enough for fish and plants to survive.

Water can also be "saline," containing large amounts of dissolved salt, or fresh, without much dissolved salt. Less than 3 percent of the water on Earth is fresh water. Almost 69 percent of that fresh water is trapped in ice and glaciers. The rest of the water on Earth is saline. Humans, and many other animals, cannot survive by drinking salt water. The dissolved salt takes more water from the human body than the water provides. Humans need fresh water to survive. However, by 2025, almost 2 billion people will live in areas without access to sources of fresh water.

Water and many ocean animals can move freely through the global ocean.

More than 3 billion people make their living from the global ocean.

By 2050, plastic in the global ocean will weigh more than the fish that live there.

The Global Ocean

Where: Earth

The vast majority of water on Earth's surface is connected through the planet's oceans, seas, rivers, and lakes. This is called the "global ocean." The global ocean formed when gas escaped from Earth and collected in the planet's atmosphere. When the gas fell back to Earth as rain, the water collected in low areas located on the surface. The Pacific Ocean is the largest and deepest body of water in the global ocean.

DISCUSSION
What steps could protect the health of the global ocean and the plants and animals that live there? Why are these steps important?

More than 200,000 species of plants and animals living in the global ocean have been identified.

The International Ice Patrol has warned ships about icebergs in the global ocean since 1914.

The global ocean helps absorb some of the greenhouse gases that may contribute to climate change.

One large tree, such as an oak, can absorb about 100 gallons (379 liters) of water out of the ground in one day.

How Plants Use Water

Plants need water to stay alive, to grow, and to produce future generations of plants. Water typically enters a plant through its roots and moves up the stem to the leaves. There, water aids the process of photosynthesis. This process turns energy from the Sun and carbon dioxide from the air into food.

Inside the plant's cells, water is also used to create pressure. When a plant does not get enough water, its stem and leaves wilt because there is not enough water pressure to hold them up. During the night, many plants release extra water from their leaves. Known as transpiration, this process creates morning dew.

Without water, a plant will eventually dry out and die. The amount of water each plant needs depends on the type of plant, where it grows, its age, and how much light it gets. Different kinds of plants survive in different environments because they have **adapted** to use water differently.

Aquatic plants live in water, with some adapted to freshwater and others to saltwater environments. Plants that live in saltwater can often break down or store salt. Estuaries are habitats where fresh water and saltwater meet. Some plants, such as cattails and mangroves, grow in estuaries because they can filter salt from the water they take in.

The saguaro cactus, found in the Sonoran Desert in the southern United States, can store up to 200 gallons (757 L) of water.

Other plants need very specific growing conditions. Cacti survive in deserts with very little water. They grow slowly to save water. Cacti also store water in their stems until they need it. Plants known as **epiphytes** grow on other plants. Their roots are exposed to the air and their leaves are designed to collect rain, dew and fog. In the rainforests of Costa Rica and the old-growth forests of North America, epiphytes often grow on plants far above the forest floor. This allows them to easily get water from the air.

The **saguaro cactus** takes **10 years** to grow **1 inch** (2.5 cm).

Forests in **North America** have more than **125 species** of **epiphytes**.

Mangrove roots can filter out about **90 percent** of the **salt in ocean water**.

How Animals Use Water

Many mammals, such as horses, lose water through breathing, sweating, and digestion.

Every single cell in an animal's body needs water to work properly. All animals get dehydrated if they do not take in enough water. Dehydration reduces the amount of blood available to carry nutrients to cells. This can cause the body's organs, including the heart, kidney, and lungs, to stop working.

Water also keeps an animal's body in good working condition. It protects delicate tissues on organs such as the eyes. Water also helps keep joints moving smoothly and aids in digestion. As part of the digestive process, water helps animals get ride of waste.

How Fish Breathe Under Water

Water carries dissolved oxygen. When a fish opens its mouth, it takes in water. That water is forced through the gills, an organ with many tiny blood vessels. As water passes over these vessels, the dissolved oxygen moves from the water and into the fish's blood. At the same time, carbon dioxide leaves the fish's body and enters the water.

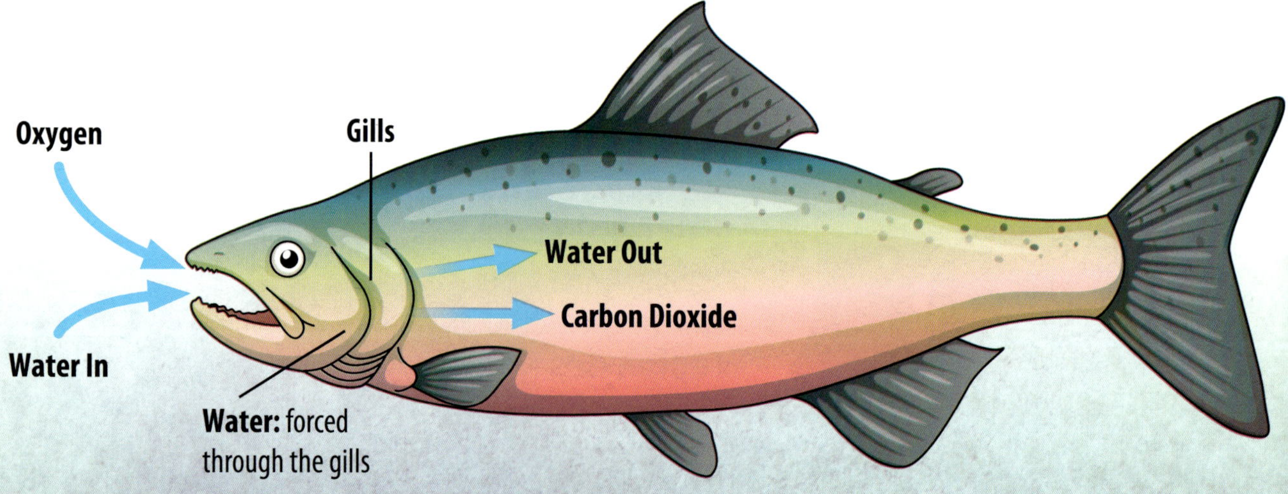

The average dog needs to drink about one ounce (30 ml) of water per pound (0.5 kg) of its body weight every day.

Animals also need water to maintain a healthy body temperature. Camels survive desert heat by drinking up to 32 gallons (121 L) of water at a time. To keep their bodies cool, hummingbirds drink two to three times their body weight every day. The ability to create sweat also helps many animals stay cool. Sweat covers the skin in moisture and gets rid of heat when it evaporates.

While all animals need to drink water, some live in it, too. Ocean animals have bodies adapted to saltwater habitats. They may be able to drink salt water, or their bodies may be able to keep the salt water out. Other animals that live in water, such as trout and perch, need fresh water to live. Salmon live part of their lives in salt water but lay their eggs in fresh water.

Other animals spend part of their lives in water. Frogs, for example, can swim but spend part of their lives on land. They lay their eggs in water because young frogs, called tadpoles, cannot survive on land. As they grow, tadpoles grow legs and lungs, allowing them to survive on the land.

How People Use Water

Water does more for people than just keeping them alive. Around the world, people use water to grow and cook their food. In developed countries, such as the United States, people also use water to brush their teeth, bathe, water their lawn, and dispose of waste. The average American home uses more than 300 gallons (1,135 L) of water every day. About 70 percent of that water is used inside the home.

Water is also essential for many common recreational and tourist activities. People travel to see glaciers, waterfalls, and beaches. Diving, fishing, boating, swimming, and luxury cruises all depend on access to water.

The United States has more than 309,000 public swimming pools.

Access to water also affects how people live and work. Firefighters use water to put out fires. Chefs use water to cook, while health professionals use clean water to help prevent the spread of diseases. Water also generates about 17 percent of the world's electricity. Businesses use water to power their offices and to cool the machines in their manufacturing plants.

For centuries, water has been used to transport goods and people. Today, about 90 percent of traded goods travel by ship. That includes items such as computers, food, and clothing.

The Panama Canal

The Panama Canal connects the Atlantic and Pacific oceans through the country of Panama. The canal is a series of chambers known as locks. Each lock is separated by metal gates powered by electricity. The locks can be flooded to lift ships across the land. Each lock is 40 feet (12 m) deep and 1,000 feet (300 m) long. Before the canal opened in 1914, ships sailing from New York to San Francisco traveled around South America. The Panama Canal cut 12,000 miles (19,000 km) from the journey. The once 67-day trip now takes 8 to 10 hours. The trip from the Atlantic to the Pacific has four key parts.

1 Atlantic Ocean

After a ship passes the first gate, the gate closes. Water from nearby lakes floods the chamber and lifts the ship above the Atlantic Ocean.

2 Gatún Lake

The ship moves from lock to lock until it reaches Gatún Lake, in the middle of the canal.

3 Miraflores Lake

The ship travels across the lake, then through another set of locks to Miraflores Lake.

4 Pacific Ocean

After Miraflores Lake, the Miraflores locks lower the ship to the Pacific Ocean.

Conserving Water Habitats

The greatest threats to the world's water habitats come from human activities. **Sewage**, pesticides, garbage, oil spills, and chemicals from factories all contaminate Earth's supply of salt and fresh water. Today, much of the world's freshwater sources are too polluted for people or animals to drink. Some fresh water is so polluted that it can no longer be used to grow food.

Plastic waste is another growing problem in water habitats. In 2017, scientists found a new patch of plastic floating in the Pacific Ocean. It is about the size of Texas.

About 9 million tons (8 million metric tons) of plastic is thrown into the ocean every year.

Greenhouse gases created when fossil fuels are burned are another problem for global ocean habitats. While the ocean absorbs these gases, doing so causes **acidification**. Acidification weakens the shells and skeletons of some marine animals, including oysters and starfish.

Scientists believe that greenhouse gases also cause climate change by trapping heat near Earth's surface. Rising air and ocean temperatures melt glaciers and polar ice and increase water acidification. Higher acidity causes coral to "bleach," or lose its color. Parts of the Great Barrier Reef, near Australia, have suffered bleaching, which leads to disease. When coral dies, many other animals lose important sources of food and their habitat.

The Great Barrier Reef is the world's largest coral reef system. It provides a habitat for more than 1,500 species of fish and 215 species of birds.

The natural cycle of water means that the total amount of water on Earth stays the same. This is a problem, since demand for water grows as the global population increases. This is why water conservation programs strive to prevent water waste and protect water quality.

Less than **one percent** of the **world's water** is available for **human use.**

Every minute, an **amount of plastic equal to a garbage truck** enters the global ocean.

Each American uses about **88 gallons** (333 L) of **water per day**.

Oceanographers

Oceanographers are scientists who study the ocean. Some oceanographers work on boats that research the plants and animals that live in the ocean. Others work in laboratories, where they study ocean chemistry and how pollution affects the habitats of plants and animals. Oceanographers also study how climate change contributes to warmer ocean currents and how these warmer currents affect global weather patterns. They use information about ocean currents and weather to predict floods, hurricanes and **droughts**.

Oceanography History

1200 BC

People living in part of what is now Israel begin using boats to ship goods from the Mediterranean to the British Isles and West Africa.

1769 AD

Benjamin Franklin publishes the first chart that maps an ocean current.

1942

The Oceans is published by a group of oceanographers. It is the first modern oceanographic reference text.

Oceanographers use a variety of tools. Scientists who study ocean currents use current maps and thermometers. That information is used to make computer models that predict major storms. Other tools let oceanographers measure salinity, acidity and oxygen levels. Some oceanographers use chemical tests to track chemicals to specific polluters.

The National Oceanic and Atmospheric Administration (NOAA) is the largest ocean research group in the United States. Established in 1970, the NOAA protects coastal areas, including beaches. It monitors the fishing industry to prevent overfishing. The organization also provides emergency managers with early warnings about storms.

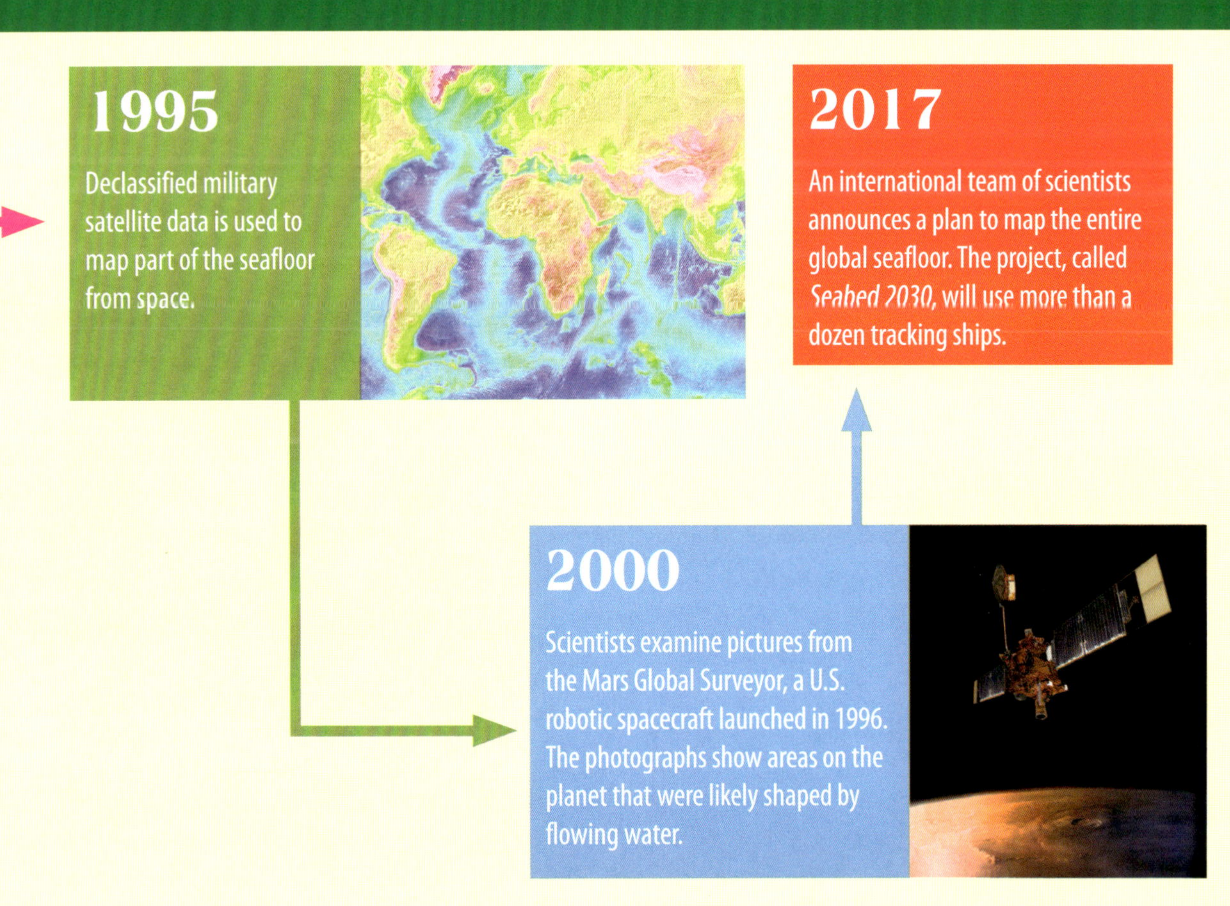

Water-Use Issues Around the World

1 California, United States

Drought affects 76 percent of the people who live in California. More than 28 million people, including millions who live in large cities such as Los Angeles, live in areas with limits on how they use water to irrigate their yards, grow food, or care for recreational spaces such as parks and golf courses.

2 Barranquilla, Colombia

Clean water is not free. In many places, such as Barranquilla, Colombia, water resources have been sold to private companies. Some people cannot afford to buy the clean water they need. Large numbers of people in locations such as Columbia, Africa, and the Philippines have to pay more for water than those who live in the United States.

3 Somali Region, Ethiopia

Climate change has reduced rainfall in several East African nations, including Ethiopia. This, along with high temperatures, makes it hard for people to grow the food they need to survive. Today, more than 8.5 million Ethiopians are at risk of starvation due to drought. In the Somali region of Ethiopia, droughts also endanger livestock herded by **nomads**.

4 Thessaloniki, Greece

In the 1930s, many marshes in northern Greece were drained so farmers could grow crops. Today, about 73 percent of those habitats are gone, including many near Thessaloniki, the capital of a region called Macedonia. Marsh plants are natural filters. Once they disappear, more agricultural pollutants enter the water.

5 Guangzhou, China

China dumps more than 90 percent of its household sewage into rivers and lakes without removing pollutants, including dangerous bacteria. Guangzhou, China's third-largest city, dumps 470,000 tons (426,000 metric tons) of untreated sewage every day. People cannot use this water to drink, wash, or grow food. In 2017, new government regulations have improved water quality in 35 heavily polluted rivers.

6 Melbourne, Australia

The population of Melbourne, Australia, is expected to double by 2065. Water providers in the city fear that demand for water may be higher than the amount available as early as 2028. The city is examining methods of recycling water from rain and storms to help meet these higher demands.

Drought Prevention and Management

People all over the world are looking for ways to manage humans, plants, and wildlife when water is scarce. Use information online and at the library to research what people and governments do to manage and prevent droughts.

WHAT HAPPENED?

Choose a country or region where a drought has taken place. Find out when it took place and how long it lasted. Was the drought caused by humans or by nature?

WHAT WAS THE EFFECT?

Look at how the drought affected the people who live in that area. Were people hurt? What did governments and organizations do to help people? Did these actions work?

WHAT ACTIONS WERE TAKEN?

Research what happened after the drought. What did people affected by it do to help manage the next dry period? Did the government do anything to make sure drought could not happen again? Were these steps successful? Why or why not?

Water Cycle Activity

Instructions

Step 1: Set the water bottle cap aside, remove labels from the bottle and cut the bottle in half.

Step 2: Moisten potting soil. Put 3 inches (8 cm) of moist potting soil mix in the bottom section of the bottle. Add the plant to the soil. Water lightly.

Step 3: Re-attach the parts of the bottle with clear packing tape.

Step 4: Replace the cap and place the bottle in the sunlight.

Step 5: Watch what happens in the bottle. Can you see moisture collecting on the side of the bottle? How does this imitate nature? What happens if you put the bottle in a dark room? Why?

Materials

Potting soil

Water

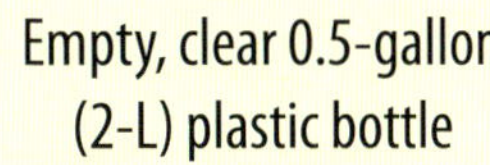

Empty, clear 0.5-gallon (2-L) plastic bottle

Small plant (such as a bean plant)

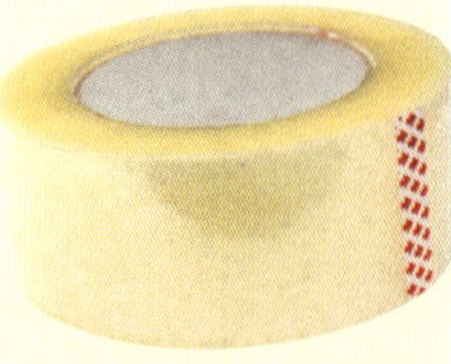

Clear packing tape

Pen and paper

Quiz

Test your knowledge by answering these questions. All of the information can be found in the text you just read. The answers are provided below for easy reference.

1. What is the chemical formula of water?

2. What is the name of the largest and deepest ocean on Earth?

3. What is the name of the lake in the middle of the Panama Canal?

4. Name the three natural states of water.

5. How much water can a camel drink at one time?

6. Name the organ fish use to breathe in oxygen from the water.

7. What percent of the Earth's surface is covered by water in its liquid form?

8. How many years can it take a saguaro cactus to grow one inch?

9. How much plastic is floating in the global ocean?

10. How much of the world's water is available for human use?

ANSWER KEY

1. H_2O **2.** The Pacific Ocean **3.** Gatún Lake **4.** Liquid, solid, gas **5.** 32 gallons (121 liters) **6.** Gills **7.** 70 **8.** 10 **9.** 9 million tons (8 million metric tons) **10.** Less than one percent

Key Words

acidification: to increase the acidity of a substance

adapted: in biology, the process of changing to survive in a new habitat or new habitat conditions

atoms: the smallest parts of an element

droughts: long periods of high heat with little to no rain

elements: the simplest part of a substance where all of the atoms are the same

epiphytes: plants that get most of their water from the air or rain, not from their roots. They usually grow on other plants.

evaporates: to change into a gas or vapor

insulates: to protect from the transfer of heat or cold

molecule: the smallest part of a substance

nomads: people who herd livestock from place to place, often in search of water

sewage: water that includes human waste

transparent: allows light to travel through

Index

LIGHTBOX

SUPPLEMENTARY RESOURCES

Click on the plus icon found in the bottom left corner of each spread to open additional teacher resources.

- Download and print the book's quizzes and activities
- Access curriculum correlations
- Explore additional web applications that enhance the Lightbox experience

LIGHTBOX DIGITAL TITLES

Packed full of integrated media

VIDEOS

INTERACTIVE MAPS

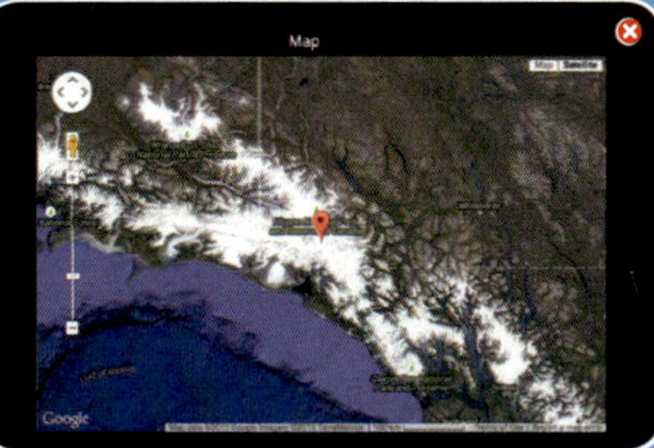

WEBLINKS

SLIDESHOWS

QUIZZES

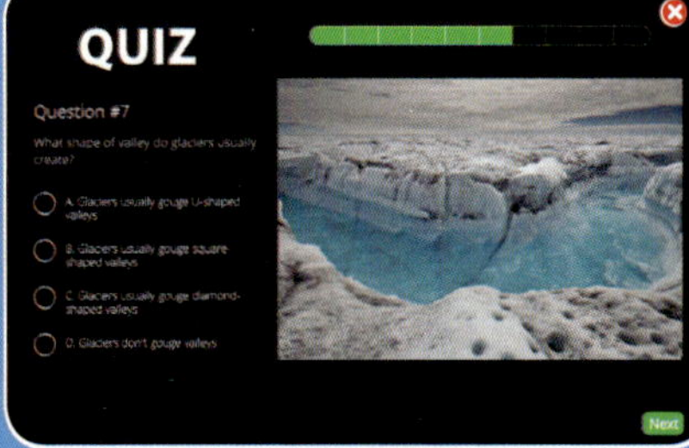

OPTIMIZED FOR

- ✓ TABLETS
- ✓ WHITEBOARDS
- ✓ COMPUTERS
- ✓ AND MUCH MORE!

Published by Smartbook Media Inc.
350 5th Avenue, 59th Floor
New York, NY 10118
Website: www.openlightbox.com

Library of Congress Control Number: 2018944572

ISBN 978-1-5105-3883-2 (hardcover)
ISBN 978-1-5105-3884-9 (multi-user eBook)

Printed in Brainerd, Minnesota, United States
1 2 3 4 5 6 7 8 9 0 22 21 20 19 18

072018
120517

Project Coordinator John Willis
Art Director Terry Paulhus

Photo Credits
Every reasonable effort has been made to trace ownership and to obtain permission to reprint copyright material. The publisher would be pleased to have any errors or omissions brought to its attention so that they may be corrected in subsequent printings. The publisher acknowledges Alamy, Getty Images, iStock, and Shutterstock as its primary image suppliers for this title.